Learn Spanish Curse Words Vulgar Expressions Includes Bonus Romantic Phrases Section

By Patrick Jackson

Copyright © 2022 Multilingual Learning, LLC

All rights reserved

No part of this publication may be reproduced, stored in a retrieval system or transmitted in any form or by any means without the prior permission in writing of the publisher, nor be circulated in writing of any publisher, nor be otherwise circulated in any form of binding or cover other than that in which it is published without a similar condition including this condition, being imposed on the subsequent purchaser.

MY WAY OF SAYING GRACIAS TO YOU

In order to say "gracias" to you for investing in this book, I have two very special bonus gifts for you.

One, I have over 5 hours of FREE MP3 audio and video Spanish lessons for you. To get access to your FREE Spanish lessons, go to: www.LearningSpanishLikeCrazy.com/webinar

Two, an invitation to attend our LIVE and INTERACTIVE monthly learning-Spanish webinars taught by an experienced Spanish instructor. I am sure that you will enjoy our webinars and learn a ton of Spanish. At the end of our Webinars, we always open up the lines and allow you to orally answer some questions or exercises in Spanish from our Spanish instructor who teaches the Webinars. This allows her to help you by checking your Spanish grammar, vocabulary and pronunciation. If you are feeling too shy to participate, you can always just listen and take notes. And if for some reason you are unable to attend a Webinar, we record the Webinars which makes it possible to send you the link to the recorded Webinar so that you can listen to it at your convenience. To sign-up and to get your FREE invitation to start attending our LIVE webinars, go to: www.LearningSpanishLikeCrazy.com/webinar

WHY DID I CREATE THIS BOOK?

Countless customers have asked me is there a book or product that will teach them swear words in Spanish. The majority of them have no interest in ever using vulgar words or phrases in Spanish but simply want to be able to understand all areas of Spanish, including curse words or other vulgar expressions.

Since there wasn't a book or product on the market that addressed this area of learning Spanish, I decided to create one.
Although I have lived in Medellin, Colombia since 2008, this book is not a book of only Colombian swear words. With the assistance of Spanish teachers from many different Spanish speaking countries, I was able to incorporate swear words from various Spanish-speaking countries, and not just Colombia.

BEFORE WE GET STARTED

The ebook and paperback books are intended to be used as a supplement for the audiobook **Learn Spanish Curse Words and Vulgar Expressions**. This book is NOT intended to be a replacement for the audiobook. Please go to Audible.com to get the audiobook for free with a trial membership to Audible.com.

TABLE OF CONTENTS

MY WAY OF SAYING GRACIAS TO YOU	3
WHY DID I CREATE THIS BOOK?	4
SPANISH CURSE WORDS IN GENERAL	7
COLOMBIAN CURSE WORDS	16
VENEZUELAN CURSE WORDS	23
ARGENTINIAN CURSE WORDS	27
MEXICAN CURSE WORDS	30
PUERTO RICAN CURSE WORDS	32
CHILEAN CURSE WORDS	35
DOMINICAN CURSE WORDS	37
VULGAR SEXUAL PHRASES	40
ROMANTIC PHRASES	42
DON'T FORGET YOUR BONUS GIFT!	50
SOME OTHER BOOKS BY THE AUTHOR	51
ABOUT THE AUTHOR	52

SPANISH CURSE WORDS IN GENERAL

1) son of a bitch – hijo de perra
Her ex-husband is a son of a bitch!
¡Su ex esposo es un hijo de puta!

2) whore – puta
My ex-wife is a whore!
¡Mi ex esposa es una puta!

3) bitch – perra
Don't be such a bitch!
¡No seas tan perra!

4) slut – zorra
That slut stole my boyfriend.
Esa zorra me robó a mi novio.

5) bastard – malparido
That bastard owes me money!
¡Ese malparido me debe dinero!

6) ass – culo
Stick it up your ass!
¡Métaselo por el culo!

7) shit – mierda
That shit is useless!
¡Esa mierda no sirve!

8) imbecile – imbécil
Only an imbecile would believe that.
Hay que ser muy imbécil para creer eso.

9) idiot – idiota
I don't like that idiot.
Ese idiota me cae mal.

10) dick face – cara de verga
Hey, dick face, give me my money!
¡Oiga, cara de verga, págueme lo que me debe!

11) retard – tarado
That retard didn't do what I told him.
Ese tarado no hizo lo que le dije.

12) dumb – tonto
You're so dumb for getting back together with her.
Eres un tonto por volver con ella.

13) fool – bobo
Hey, fool, I'm talking to you!
¡Oiga, bobo, le estoy hablando!

14) stupid – estúpido
You're so stupid for not going to the party.
Eres un estúpido por no ir a la fiesta.

15) hooker – ramera
That one is a filthy hooker!
¡Esa es una ramera asquerosa!

16) devil – diablo
Go to the devil!
¡Vete al diablo!

17) whore – golfa
I hate that whore.
Odio a esa golfa.

18) fool – zopenco
That fool doesn't know what he's talking about.
Ese zopenco no sabe de qué habla.

19) fool – zoquete
A fool like him will never be successful.
Un zoquete como él nunca va a tener éxito.

20) simpleton – mentecato
Any simpleton can do that.
Cualquier mentecato puede hacer eso.

21) prick – huevón
That prick is useless.
Ese huevón no sirve para nada.

22) balls – huevas
Eat my balls!
¡Cómase mis huevas!

23) fucker – cabrón
Leave me alone, fucker!
¡Déjeme quieto, cabrón!

24) fuck you – jódete
Fuck you, leave me alone!
¡Jódete, no me molestes más!

25) asshole – pirobo
What's your problem, asshole?
¿Qué le pasa, pirobo?

26) scruffy – zarrapastroso
Don't let that scruffy guy enter my restaurant!
¡No dejen entrar a ese zarrapastroso a mi restaurante!

27) dumb – sonso
You're so dumb, you better study.
Usted es muy sonso, vaya estudie mejor.

28) despicable – piltrafa
Such a despicable person like you doesn't deserve anything.
Una piltrafa como usted no se merece nada.

29) dummy – pelele
You're such a useless dummy!
¡Eres un pelele bueno para nada!

30) ragamuffin – pelagato
That ragamuffin is a drug addict.
Ese pelagato es un drogadicto.

31) sucker – papanatas
I'm going to fire that useless sucker!
¡Voy a despedir a ese papanatas inútil!

32) fool – majadero
Only a fool would believe that story.
Solamente un majadero se creería esa historia.

33) bootlicker – lameculos
I'm done with that bootlicker!
¡Estoy harto de ese lameculos!

34) jerk – cretino
You're such a jerk!
¡Eres un cretino!

35) assface – caraculo
Hey, assface, bring me that!
¡Oye, caraculo, tráeme eso!

36) brute – cafre
That guy is an impolite brute.
Ese tipo es un cafre mal educado.

37) idiot – bobalicón
I was such an idiot back in high-school.
Yo era un bobalicón en el colegio.

38) scoundrel – bellaco
You're such a lying scoundrel!
¡Eres un bellaco mentiroso!

39) fag – marica
Don't be such a fag!
¡No seas marica!

40) faggot – maricón
You're a fucking faggot!
¡Eres un maldito maricón!

41) trashy – guisa
You're so trashy and awful.
Eres una guisa horrible.

42) slut – zunga
That slut is dating a married man.
Esa zunga está saliendo con un hombre casado.

43) crap – cagar
I have to take a crap.
Tengo que cagar.

44) wimp – cagón
Don't be such a wimp, the water is not that cold!
¡No seas tan cagón, el agua no está tan fría!

45) fuck-up – cagada
I don't think I'll get the job after that fuck-up I made.
No creo que consiga el trabajo después de esa cagada que cometí.

46) fuck – coño
Fuck, I forgot the homework!
¡Coño, olvidé la tarea!

47) ball sucker – mamahuevo
That ball sucker is not going to beat me.
Ese mamahuevo no me va a ganar.

48) to screw up – joder
Don't screw it up!
¡No lo vayas a joder!

49) to cum – venirse
I came in your wife's face.
Me vine en la cara de tu esposa.

50) fucker – maldito
I hate that fucker!
¡Odio a ese maldito!

51) scumbag – pichurria
That guy is a scumbag!
¡Ese tipo es una pichurria!

52) pussy – pendejo
Why are you such a pussy?
¿Por qué eres tan pendejo?

53) ugly – feo
Your wife is very ugly.
Tu mujer es muy fea.

54) dog – perro
He's a fucking dog!
¡Él es un maldito perro!

55) wretch – desgraciado
Shut up, wretch!
¡Cállate, desgraciado!

56) dumbass – ahuevonado
He stole your girlfriend because you're such a dumbass.
Por ahuevonado te quitó a tu novia.

57) bastard – bastardo
You fucking bastard!
¡Maldito bastardo!

58) your mother – tu mamá
Your mother is a slut.
Tu mamá es una perra.

59) wuss – culero
You're such a coward wuss!
¡Eres un culero cobarde!

COLOMBIAN CURSE WORDS

60) gonorrhea – gonorrea
What's your problem, gonorrhea?
¿Qué le pasa, gonorrea?

61) angry – emputado
I'm so angry!
¡Estoy muy emputado!

62) dick – mondá
Go eat 3 kilos of dick!
¡Cómete tres kilos de mondá!

63) blowjob – mamada
Give me a blowjob!
¡Deme una mamada!

64) motherfucker – malparido
You're a heartless motherfucker!
¡Usted es un malparido sin sentimientos!

65) trashy – ñero
That trashy guy is going to mug me.
Ese ñero me va a robar.

66) tacky – loba
That girl is so tacky.
Esa vieja es una loba.

67) asshole – pirobo
I don't like that asshole.
Ese pirobo me cae mal.

68) dick face – caremondá
Fight me, you dick face!
¡Vamos a pelear, caremondá!

69) horny – arrecho
That girl makes me so horny.
Esa vieja me pone muy arrecho.

70) cheap – líchigo
Don't be so cheap, pay the bill.
No sea líchigo, pague la cuenta.

71) fool – bobo
That's wrong, you big fool.
Gran bobo, eso está mal hecho.

72) fuck off – ábrase
Fuck off, I don't want to see you!
¡Ábrase que no lo quiero ver!

73) fag – loca
What a fag, drink a shot!
¡Qué loca, tómese un trago!

74) faggot – locota
What a faggot, go talk to her!
¡Qué locota, háblele a esa vieja!

75) gossipy – sapo
Go away, don't be so gossipy!
¡Váyase, no sea sapo!

76) idiot – pingo
Don't be such an idiot!
¡No sea tan pingo!

77) pussy – pendejo
What a pussy!
¡Qué pendejo!

78) pee – mear
I need to pee so bad!
¡Tengo muchas ganas de mear!

79) poop – cagar
I need to poop so bad!
¡Tengo muchas ganas de cagar!

80) lame – simplón
What a boring and lame guy!
¡Qué tipo tan aburrido y simplón!

81) scumbag – pichurria
That guy is a scumbag!
¡Ese tipo es una pichurria!

82) pig – cerdo
Gross, don't be such a pig!
¡Qué asco, no sea tan cerdo!

83) prick – huevón
Pay attention, you prick!
¡Ponga atención, huevón!

84) cheap – chichipato
Why are you so cheap?
¿Usted por qué es tan chichipato?

85) bitch – grilla
That girl is such a bitch!
¡Esa vieja es una grilla!

86) bitch – perra
What's your problem, bitch?
¿Qué le pasa, perra?

87) tacky – corroncho
You look so tacky with those colorful shoes!
¡Te ves muy corroncho con esos zapatos de colores!

88) fuck – culear
Today I'm going to fuck her.
Hoy voy a culear con ella.

89) fuck – tirar
We're going to fuck tonight!
¡Esta noche vamos a tirar!

90) whore – guaricha
They told me she was a whore.
Me dijeron que ella era una guaricha.

91) motherfucker – malnacido
That motherfucker is going to pay me!
¡Ese malnacido me va a pagar!

92) faggot – cacorro
That guy is a faggot!
¡Ese tipo es un cacorro!

93) dickface – carechimba
I'm going to kill that dickface!
¡Voy a matar a ese carechimba!

94) garbage – bazofia
That piece of garbage deserves nothing!
¡Esa bazofia no se merece nada!

95) shit – mierda
You big piece of shit!
¡Grandísimo pedazo de mierda!

96) annoying – petardo
That guy is so annoying!
¡Ese tipo es un petardo!

97) ass face – careculo
Hey, ass face, come here.
¡Oye, careculo, ven para acá!

98) dyke – arepera
That girl is such a dyke.
Esa vieja es una arepera.

99) fucker – cabrón
Stop being such a fucker!
¡Deja de ser tan cabrón!

100) whore – patialegre
She's such a whore when she's drunk.
Ella se pone patialegre cuando está borracha.

101) sucker – mamón
I can't stand that sucker!
¡No soporto a ese mamón!

102) suck dick – mámelo
Go suck dick!
¡Vaya mámelo!

103) pussy – cuca
Stick your apologies up your pussy!
¡Métase sus disculpas por la cuca!

104) ass – culo
Stick it up your ass!
¡Métaselo por el culo!

105) son of a bitch – hijueputa
You are the dumbest son of a bitch in the world.
Eres el hijueputa más bobo del mundo..

VENEZUELAN CURSE WORDS

106) angry – arrecho
That guy is making me angry!
¡Ese tipo ya me tiene arrecho!

107) clumsy – babieco
That clumsy guy fell off the bed!
¡Ese babieco se cayó de la cama!

108) dyke – cachapera
Your friend is a dyke!
¡Tu amiga es una cachapera!

109) shitty – cagalitroso
What a shitty dude!
¡Qué tipo tan cagalitroso!

110) fuck – coger
I'll fuck her tonight!
¡Esta noche me la voy a coger!

111) bootlicker – chupaculo
I don't like bootlickers.
No me caen bien los chupaculos.

112) fuck – coño
Fuck, leave me alone!
¡Coño, déjame en paz!

113) bitch – cuaima
Your wife is such a bitch!
¡Tu esposa es tremenda cuaima!

114) arrogant – comemierda
That guy is so arrogant!
¡Ese tipo es un comemierda!

115) annoying – ladilla
You're so annoying!
¡Eres una ladilla!

116) stingy – lambucio
Share some, don't be so stingy!
¡Comparte, no seas lambucio!

117) motherfucker – malparido
I hate you, motherfucker!
¡Te odio, malparido!

118) ball sucker – mamahuevo
That ball sucker is going to regret it!
¡Ese mamahuevo se va a arrepentir!

119) fag – marico
I don't like that fag.
No me cae bien ese marico.

120) liar – mojonero
Stop being such a liar!
¡Deja de ser tan mojonero!

121) faggot – muerde almohadas
Your boyfriend is a faggot!
¡Tu novio es un muerde almohadas!

122) snitch – pajúo
That snitch gave me away!
¡Ese pajúo me delató!

123) pussy – papo
Suck my pussy!
¡Chúpame el papo!

124) fag – pargo
Stop being such a fag!
¡Deja de ser tan pargo!

125) pussy – pocha
You have a filthy pussy!
¡Tienes la pocha sucia!

126) whore – puta
What a whore!
¡Qué vieja tan puta!

127) horny – quesúo
I'm so horny!
¡Estoy quesúo!

128) stupid – tarúpido
That guy is so stupid!
¡Ese tipo es un gran tarúpido!

129) dick – verga
Suck my dick!
¡Chúpame la verga!

ARGENTINIAN CURSE WORDS

130) asshole – boludo
Don't be such an asshole!
¡No seas tan boludo!

131) pussy – concha
Your mom's pussy!
¡La concha de tu madre!

132) ass – orto
Stick it up your ass!
¡Métetelo por el orto!

133) idiot – pajero
That idiot is useless!
¡Ese pajero es un inservible!

134) dick – pija
Suck my dick!
¡Chúpame la pija!

135) son of a bitch – hijo de puta
I will kill you, son of a bitch!
¡Te voy a matar, hijo de puta!

136) asshole – pelotudo
You're an asshole!
¡Sos un pelotudo!

137) balls – huevos
Suck my balls!
¡Chúpame los huevos!

138) butt – ojete
Stick it up your butt!
¡Métetelo por el ojete!

139) dyke – tortillera
Your girlfriend is a dyke!
¡Tu novia es una tortillera!

140) fuck – clavar
I will fuck her tonight!
¡Esta noche me la voy a clavar!

141) asshole – forro
You're such an asshole!
¡Qué forro sos!

142) blowjob – pete
Give me a blowjob!
¡Haceme un pete!

143) despicable – sorete
That guy is despicable.
Ese tipo es un sorete.

144) fuck – garchar
I will fuck her later!
¡Me la voy a garchar más tarde!

145) dick – poronga
¡Chúpame la poronga!
Suck my dick!

146) faggot – trabuco
Look at that faggot!
¡Mira a ese Trabuco!

147) idiot – gil
You're an idiot!
¡Sos un gil!

MEXICAN CURSE WORDS

148) stupid – pendejo
Why are you so stupid?
¿Por qué eres tan pendejo?

149) fag – puto
Your husband is a fag!
¡Tu marido es un puto!

150) bother – chingar
Stop bothering me!
¡Deja de chingar!

151) fucker – cabrón
You're a damn fucker!
¡Eres un maldito cabrón!

152) asshole – culero
Don't be such an asshole, help me!
¡No seas culero, ayúdame!

153) asshole – ojete
You're such an asshole!
¡Eres un ojete!

154) faggot – joto
Juan is a faggot!
¡Juan es un joto!

155) hell – chingada
Go to hell!
¡Vete a la chingada!

156) angry – encabronado
I'm so angry!
¡Estoy muy encabronado!

157) ass – burro
You're an ass!
¡Eres un burro!

158) asshole – baboso
Camilo is an asshole!
¡Camilo es un baboso!

159) idiot – tarado
My Little brother is an idiot!
¡Mi hermanito es un tarado!

PUERTO RICAN CURSE WORDS

160) dick – bicho
Suck my dick!
¡Chúpame el bicho!

161) balls – bolas
Suck my balls!
¡Chúpame las bolas!

162) Dyke – bucha
Your mom is a dyke!
¡Tu mama es una bucha!

163) liar – buchipluma
You're a damn liar!
¡Eres un maldito buchipluma!

164) faggot – bugarón
Your boyfriend is a faggot!
¡Tu novio es un bugarón!

165) fucker – cabrón
That guy is a fucker!
¡Ese tipo es un cabrón!

166) dyke – cachapera
Your sister is a dyke!
¡Tu Hermana es cachapera!

167) fuck – chichar
I want to fuck with her!
¡Quiero chichar con ella!

168) fuck – chingar
I will fuck you!
¡Te voy a chingar!

169) whore – cochofle
That woman is a whore!
¡Esa mujer es un cochofle!

170) pussy – crica
I want to suck her pussy!
¡Le quiero chupar la crica!

171) dick – mamerro
You want my dick!
¡Tu quieres mi mamerro!

172) faggot – maricón
You're a faggot!
¡Eres un maricón!

173)   shit – Mojón
You're a piece of shit!
¡Eres un pedazo de mojón!

174)   fuck – singar
I will fuck her!
¡A ella me la voy a singar!

CHILEAN CURSE WORDS

175)   idiot – huevón
You're such an idiot!
¡Eres un huevón!

176)   fucking – culiao
That fucking laptop is not working!
¡Ese computador culiao no sirve!

177)   hell – chucha
Go to hell and leave me alone!
¡Vete a la chucha y déjame en paz!

178)   whore – maraca
My ex-girlfriend is a whore.
Mi ex novia es una maraca.

179)   fuck – culiar
I want to fuck tonight!
¡Tengo ganas de culiar esta noche!

180)   shit – mierda
Go eat shit!
¡Ve a comer mierda!

181) dumbass – ahuevonado
You're such a dumbass!
¡Eres un ahuevonado!

182) clumsy – gil
He's so clumsy he doesn't even know where to go!
¡Es tan gil que no sabe a dónde ir!

183) faggot – maricón
Don't be such a faggot!
¡No seas tan maricón!

184) dick – pico
Suck my dick!
¡Chúpame el pico!

185) fuck – garchar
I'm going to fuck my girlfriend!
¡Voy a garchar con mi novia!

186) dick – pichula
Do you want to see my dick?
¿Me quieres ver la pichula?

DOMINICAN CURSE WORDS

187)　idiot – aciguatado
That kid is an idiot!
¡Ese niño es un aciguatado!

188)　pain in the ass – afrentoso
My little brother is a pain in the ass!
¡Mi hermanito es un afrentoso!

189)　dyke – machorra
You're a dyke!
¡Eres una machorra!

190)　dick – ñema
Suck my dick!
¡Chúpame la ñema!

191)　pussy – toto
I want to suck your pussy!
¡Quiero chuparte el toto!

192)　fuck – singar
I know you want to fuck me!
¡Yo sé que tú quieres singar conmigo!

193) ball sucker – mamahuevo
You're a ball sucker for leaving!
¡Eres un mamahuevo por irte!

194) bitch – perra
That bitch stole my wife!
¡Esa perra me robó mi esposa!

195) fucker – cabrón
You are a fucker!
¡Tú lo que eres es un cabrón!

196) asshole – huevón
Who's that asshole?
¿Quién es ese huevón?

197) motherfucker – malnacido
That motherfucker doesn't know who I am.
Ese malnacido no me conoce.

198) shit – mierda
I don't give a shit!
¡Me vale mierda!

199) faggot – maricón
Are you a faggot, or what?
¿Acaso eres maricón?

200) ass – culo
I will stick it up your ass!
¡Te lo voy a meter por el culo!

201) idiot – boquechivo
That idiot can't do anything right!
¡Ese boquechivo no hace nada bien!

VULGAR SEXUAL PHRASES

202) sixty-nine – el sesenta y nueve
This position is better than a 69.
Esta posición es mejor que un sesenta y nueve.

203) tit, boob- teta
I want to come on your tits.
Quiero venirme en tus tetas.

204) to put it in, to stick it in – meter
Put it in my mouth.
Métemela en la boca.

205) ass, asshole – culo
I want you to fuck me in the ass.
Quiero que me cojas por el culo.

206) hard – duro
I want you to fuck me hard.
Quiero que me cojas duro.

207) cum – leche, lechita
I want to swallow your cum.
Quiero tragarme tu leche.

208) doggy style – en cuatro, posición del perrito
I want to fuck you doggy-style.
Quiero cogerte en cuatro.

209) missionary position – postura del misionero
I want you to fuck me missionary style.
Quiero que me cojas en la posición del misionero.

210) pussy – chocha
I want to suck your pussy.
Te quiero mamar la chocha.

211) threesome – trio
I want to have a threesome.
Quiero hacer un trio.

ROMANTIC PHRASES

1) love – amor
You are my love.
Eres mi amor.

2) honey – cariño
Honey, you're the best thing in my life.
Cariño, eres lo mejor de mi vida.

3) baby – bebé
Baby, I love you.
Bebé, te amo.

4) in love – enamorado, enamorada
I think I'm in love with you.
Creo que estoy enamorado de ti

5) adore – adorar
I adore you with all that I am.
Te adoro con todo lo que soy.

6) like – gustar
I really like you a lot.
En verdad me gustas mucho.

7) like – querer
I like you as more than just a friend.
Te quiero como algo más que un amigo.

8) beautiful – bonita/o
You are the most beautiful woman in the world.
Eres la mujer más bonita del mundo.

9) cute – lindo, linda
My boyfriend is so cute.
Mi novio es muy lindo.

10) gorgeous – hermosa, hermoso
She is the most gorgeous in school.
Ella es la más linda de la escuela.

11) to kiss – besar
I want to kiss those lips forever.
Quiero besar esos labios por siempre.

12) hug- abrazar
Just a hug from you makes everything ok.
Un abrazo tuyo hace que todo esté bien.

13) boyfriend – novio
You are the best boyfriend in the world.
Eres el mejor novio del mundo.

14) girlfriend – novia
Do you want to be my girlfriend?
¿Quieres ser mi novia?

15) miss – extrañar
I miss you every time you leave the house.
Te extraño cada vez que te vas.

16) crazy – loco, loca
I'm crazy about you.
Estoy loco por ti.

17) pretty – bella, bello
You have such pretty eyes.
Tienes unos ojos muy bellos.

18) love – amar
I will love you forever.
Te voy a amar por siempre.

19) sweetheart – querido, querida
It's good to see you, sweetheart.
Me encanta verte, querida.

20) heart – corazón
You make my heart beat fast.
Haces que mi corazón lata rápido.

21) princess – princesa
You are my princess.
Eres mi princesa.

22) queen – reina
You are the queen of my heart.
Eres la reina de mi corazón.

23) crush – flechado, flechada
I think I have a crush on you.
Creo que me tienes flechada.

24) heaven – cielo
You are heaven to me.
Eres mi cielo.

25) to smile, smile – sonreir, sonrisa
You make me smile.
Me haces sonreír.

26) precious – preciosa, precioso
You are the most precious girl in the universe.
Eres la chica más preciosa del universo.

27) heavenly – divino, divina
You are a heavenly human being.
Eres un ser humano divino.

28) handsome – guapo
You are the most handsome husband.
Eres el esposo más guapo.

29) adorable – adorable
You look adorable when you smile.
Te ves adorable cuando sonríes.

30) my life – mi vida
My life, you are the best.
Mi vida, eres la mejor.

31) baby – nena, nene
Baby, I love you.
Nena, te amo.

32) doll – muñeca
You are my doll.
Eres mi muñeca.

33) shorty – chiquita
How is my shorty doing today?
¿Cómo está mi Chiquita hoy?

34) teddy bear – osito, osita
He's tender like a teddy bear.
Él es tierno como un osito.

35) little thing – cosita
I really like you, little thing.
Me encantas, cosita.

36) cutie – hermosura
You are a cutie, did you know that?
¿Sabías que eres una hermosura?

37) beauty – preciosura
You are such a beauty.
Eres una preciosura.

38) beauty – belleza
Your beauty hypnotizes me.
Tu belleza me hipnotiza.

39) passion – pasión
You awaken all of my passions.
Despiertas todas mis pasiones.

40) my everything – mi todo
You are my everything.
Eres mi todo.

41) charming – encantador
You are a charming man.
Eres un hombre encantador.

42) spoon – arrunchar
Come spoon me!
¡Ven y me arrunchas!

43) loving, affectionate – tierno
My love, you are very affectionate.
Mi amor, eres muy tierna.

44) marriage – matrimonio
Our marriage is a holy contract.
Nuestro matrimonio es un contrato sagrado.

45) to get married – casarse
Would you marry me?
¿Te quieres casar conmigo?

46) beloved – amado, amada
I can't believe you are my beloved husband.
No puedo creer que tú seas mi amado esposo.

47) adored – adorado, adorada
My adored wife, I will love you forever.
Adorada esposa, te voy a amar por siempre.

48) treasure – tesoro
You are my most valuable treasure.
Eres mi tesoro más preciado.

49) flirt – coquetear
I love it when you flirt with me.
Me encanta cuando me coqueteas.

50) cuddle – apapachar
I want you to cuddle me.
Quiero que me apapaches.

51) to spoil – mimar
Today I want to spoil you all day long.
Hoy quiero mimarte todo el día.

DON'T FORGET YOUR BONUS GIFT!

In order to say "gracias" to you for investing in this book, I have two very special bonus gifts for you.

One, I have over 5 hours of FREE MP3 audio and video Spanish lessons for you. To get access to your FREE Spanish lessons, go to:

www.LearningSpanishLikeCrazy.com/webinar

Two, an invitation to attend our LIVE and INTERACTIVE monthly learning-Spanish webinars taught by an experienced Spanish instructor. I am sure that you will enjoy our webinars and learn a ton of Spanish. At the end of our Webinars, we always open up the lines and allow you to orally answer some questions or exercises in Spanish from our Spanish instructor who teaches the Webinars. This allows her to help you by checking your Spanish grammar, vocabulary and pronunciation. If you are feeling too shy to participate, you can always just listen and take notes. And if for some reason you are unable to attend a Webinar, we record the Webinars which makes it possible to send you the link to the recorded Webinar so that you can listen to it at your convenience. To sign-up and to get your FREE invitation to start attending our LIVE webinars, go to:

www.LearningSpanishLikeCrazy.com/webinar

SOME OTHER BOOKS BY THE AUTHOR

Avoid 100 Plus Gringo Mistakes – NEW & Improved Edition Includes Quizzes

This book covers the most common Spanish-speaking mistakes native English speakers make when speaking Spanish. 100 Plus Gringo Mistakes also explains why native English speakers tend to commit such errors. Your new understanding of why you make such mistakes will help you to avoid these pitfalls while enabling you to master conversational Spanish.

Learn Spanish Curse Words and Vulgar Expressions (Audiobook)

The ebook and paperback books are intended to be used as a supplement for the audiobook *Learn Spanish Curse Words and Vulgar Expressions*. This book is NOT intended to be a replacement for the audiobook. Please go to Audible.com to get the audiobook for free with a trial membership to Audible.com.

ABOUT THE AUTHOR

Patrick Jackson is a native New Yorker and a retired attorney. He received his J.D. (Juris Doctor) from Georgetown University Law Center. He is also the Founder of *Learning Like Crazy*, a company that has created the following products:

- Learning Spanish Like Crazy
- Verbarrator (Spanish verb conjugation software)
- Learning Portuguese Like Crazy
- Learning Italian Like Crazy

He travels the world throughout the year but prefers to spend half the year in Medellin, Colombia, *"La Ciudad de la Eterna Primavera"* (The City of Eternal Spring).

Printed in Great Britain
by Amazon